MILLIONAIRE SHORTCUT

WHO YOU NEED TO BE
(AND WHAT YOU NEED TO SELL):

FOR FRUSTRATED INTERNET ENTREPRENEURS
THAT WANT TO LIVE RICH FOR A LIFETIME

RICHARD G. LEWIS

Download a FREE Millionaire Shortcut Cheat Sheet here:

https://richardglewis.com/millionaire-shortcut-cheatsheet

Copyright © 2021 Present Riana Publishing

All rights reserved.

Copyright © Riana Publishing 2021

The right of Riana Publishing to be identified as the author of this work has been asserted by the company in accordance with the Copyrights, Designs and Patents Act 1988.

All rights reserved.

Published by Riana Publishing a division of The Riana Group Palmdale CA 93551 USA

All rights reserved. No part of this publication may be reproduced, stored in a retrieval system, or transmitted in any form or by any means - for example, electronic, photocopy, recording - without the prior written permission of the publisher. The only exception is brief quotations in printed reviews.

TABLE OF CONTENTS

EARNINGS AND INCOME DISCLAIMER 7
PREFACE 9
FINDING A PROFITABLE NICHE 11
DEFINITIONS 15
INTRODUCTION 17
CHAPTER ONE : WHY SHOULD YOU START AN ONLINE BUSINESS? 19
    IN THE PLACE TO BE 21
    THE INTERNET 22
    HOW TO MAKE $ERIOUS MONEY ONLINE 23
    CAN YOUR HOBBY MAKE YOU RICH? 25
    WHICH NICHE WOULD SUIT YOU? 29
CHAPTER TWO : IDEA GENERATION (IDEATION) 33
    NEVER BE THE FIRST THROUGH THE DOOR 35
    TO TEST IS BEST 36
    WHAT SHOULD YOU SELL? 37
    YOU WON'T GO FAR WITHOUT IPR 39
CHAPTER THREE : SO WHAT EXACTLY DO PEOPLE WANT? 41
    DO YOU FULFILL YOUR CUSTOMERS' NEEDS? 44
    DOES YOUR BUSINESS IDEA FIT THE INTERNET? 45
    INTERNET USAGE AMONG AMERICANS 49
    WHAT SELLS ONLINE 49
    WHAT DOESN'T SELL ONLINE 50
    HOW CAN YOU MAKE MONEY ONLINE? 51
    THE "BIG THREE" NICHES 51
CONCLUSION 53
ABOUT THE AUTHOR 55

EARNINGS AND INCOME DISCLAIMER

Every effort has been made by the author to accurately represent the potential of income from using the advice in this book.

The author offers no guarantee, whether expressed or implied, that you will earn any money using the products, publications, documents, services, techniques, advice and/or ideas suggested in this book.

The earning potential is entirely dependent on the person or organization using the author's products, services, publications, documents, advice, ideas and/or techniques.

This is not a "Get Rich Quick" scheme.

The author has no way of knowing how well you will do, as the author does not know you, your background, your work ethic, your level of commitment, your financial standing or your business skills.

The author DOES NOT guarantee, imply, or predict that you will get rich, that you will do as well as others or that you will earn any money at all.

Your level of success in attaining the results claimed or promised in the author's materials may vary.

Your success depends totally on the time and effort you devote to the program, ideas, suggestions and techniques mentioned, your knowledge, wisdom, experience, intuition, skills, efforts, behavior, education, expertise, level of desire, and individual capacity.

Since these factors and circumstances vary according to individuals, the author cannot guarantee your success, performance, or income level.

The author disclaims any and all liability, both tangible and intangible, for loss or risk incurred as a consequence of the use and application, either directly or indirectly, of any advice, information, methods and techniques presented by the author through any and all mediums - including, but not limited to, oral, visual, and written direction.

The information included in this book and any accompanying literature and products, regarding various business or marketing methods, is for information purposes only.

PREFACE

Thank you for choosing this book. I sincerely believe that if you follow my advice, you will significantly improve your chances of making $ERIOUS MONEY online.

I honestly believe that I now know as much about what works and what does not work regarding making money online as anyone in the business. I now want to share that knowledge with you.

FINDING A PROFITABLE NICHE

The purpose of this book is to help you find profitable niches - niches that will provide you with enough money to make a good living online, maybe even enough money to sponsor your dream lifestyle (like me)! There are countless undiscovered or under-exploited niches still out there, and thousands of new niches created every day.

I'll explain in detail all the techniques needed to make your online business a success, including: idea generation, market research, the *Risk Eliminator*™ system, as well as the importance of the *Keyword Continuum*™ and a *Unique Proposition Strategy*™.

Profit from Persuasion,

Richard G Lewis

Richard G. Lewis
http://www.RichardGLewis.com

DEDICATION

To My Wonderful Wife, Son, and Family.

DEFINITIONS

Niche (niCH) Noun. A small recess, gap, or space.

Niche Market. A small segment of a market suitable for focused attention by a marketer.

Niche Marketing. Concentrating marketing efforts on a small but specific and well-defined segment of the population.

Profitable Niche. A small segment of a market in which demand for a very specialized product or commodity is sufficient to enough to provide monetary surplus (left to a producer or employer after deducting wages, rent, cost of raw materials, etc.)

INTRODUCTION

It is a fact; the most likely way of making a million dollars is not by buying a lottery ticket or investing in stock or property. Other than inheriting money, the way that most people become rich is by owning a successful business. Running a business is never easy but fortune favors the brave, and the rewards can be huge.

> "YOU WILL NEVER DO ANYTHING IN THIS WORLD WITHOUT COURAGE. IT IS THE GREATEST QUALITY OF THE MIND NEXT TO HONOR."
> ARISTOTLE

Often, the hardest part about starting a business is coming up with an idea for a business or choosing a product or service. Next, more importantly, you will need to find customers that want to buy what you are selling. If you get this part of your planning wrong, it can be an extremely expensive mistake! That is why it is so important to do your research and choose the correct option.

> "THE BEGINNING IS THE MOST IMPORTANT PART OF THE WORK."
> PLATO

Using the advice, examples, case studies, techniques, and tools in this book you will learn how to significantly improve your chances of establishing a profitable online business.

By identifying a profitable niche, researching your target market, and testing your marketing message, you will be able to set realistic, achievable goals.

> "A GOAL PROPERLY SET IS HALFWAY REACHED."
> ZIG ZIGLAR

There are many reasons why people start their own business. Only you'll know if it's the right time to start a business, but it's a fact that most successful business people are not exceptionally smart – the smartest thing they ever do is take the right advice – that's the purpose of this book; to show you how to make $ERIOUS MONEY online!

If you're reading this then you know how vitally important choosing a profitable niche is, **it's the most critical part of internet marketing** - choose the right niche and overnight you could find yourself making more money than you can handle - choose the wrong niche and in just a few months from now you could be flat broke and tired out from wasting your precious resources on a bum niche!

Choosing the Right Niche is The Foundation of Everything Else You Do. These days, setting up an efficient sales funnel is easy, almost everything online can be automated, and there is enough advice about internet marketing to ensure you will do all the right things, but...

EVERYTHING DEPENDS ON YOU FIRST IDENTIFYING A PROFITABLE NICHE!

CHAPTER ONE

WHY SHOULD YOU START AN ONLINE BUSINESS?

If you are serious about securing your financial future then an online business can be the least risky, most profitable, and most enjoyable option. Furthermore, even if you are determined to create a physical bricks and mortar brand, the best place to test your concept is online.

Top Reasons Why People Start Their Own Business:

1. Freedom
2. Wealth
3. Fulfillment

Obviously, if you follow the right advice it is much more probable that you will succeed. However, we all know that it is often other qualities that determine our success or failure.

> *"The will to win, the desire to succeed, the urge to reach your full potential... these are the keys that will unlock the door to personal excellence."*
>
> *Confucius*

Rather than concentrating on the positives, very often success comes from avoiding the negative influences. Before you embark on any business venture, it is a good idea to be aware of the pitfalls you may encounter.

Top Reasons Why People Fail:

1. Business Too Dependent on Owner
2. Exhaustion
3. Not Enough Capital
4. Not Enough Expertise
5. Failure to Ask for Help
6. Distractions

Very often the best way to start a business is part time, from home, while you maintain your day job. Thousands of successful entrepreneurs and online businesspeople have started in this way; step-by-step.

"It does not matter how slowly you go as long as you do not stop."

Confucius

The important thing is to make the change as soon as possible. Seize the opportunity and start the process today; follow the advice in this book and success could be yours much quicker than you think.

"Opportunities multiply as they are seized."

Sun Tzu

IN THE PLACE TO BE

And the best place to start any business these days? On the internet. It is without exception the cheapest, most cost-effective channel to market the world of commerce has ever known. No other marketplace can offer a comparable means of accurately pre-testing or measuring your potential market share, your advertising costs, your conversion rates, your customers' usage paths, your marketing messages etc. etc. All before you risk anything.

The next few years will see a huge take up of the internet throughout the world. Most experts are predicting a 200%+ global increase in the number of internet users and broadband provision over the next three to five years as the various world economies fulfill their various economic 'stimulation packages' by providing the infrastructure for fast internet usage. This will provide the biggest retail audience the world has ever seen, all in one place, all accessible by you.

Thanks to the internet, for the very first time an individual or micro business can compete on the same level playing field as a huge global brand. If you can provide a high-quality product or service to a niche target market (backed up with good customer service and delivery, added value, and exceptional product knowledge), you can make $ERIOUS MONEY online.

THE INTERNET

If you are serious about starting a business that can make lots of money quickly, then the internet is the place to be. Compared to any other channel to market in history the internet is the cheapest in which to test, set-up, launch, maintain, market, and grow your business.

There are currently over 6 million small businesses in the United States and, based on what you hear in the news and by talking with others, you might assume that everyone who has a business also has a website for e-commerce. Amazingly, the truth is that approximately 67.8% of small businesses **do not** sell any products or services online. What an opportunity to step in and dominate your chosen market sector!

By 2022, e-retail revenues will grow to $6.54 trillion, up from $3.53 trillion in 2019.

In 2021, voice commerce, omnichannel shopping, AI, and AR will likely be prevalent, and more online businesses will have to accept crypto payments.

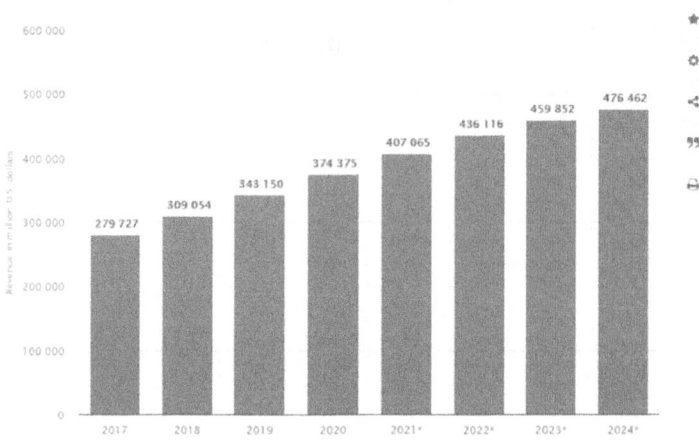

The Web is only 20 years old; it is still in its infancy. The time to start your business is now, or else you will regret it every time you see someone else making serious money online.

HOW TO MAKE $ERIOUS MONEY ONLINE

Here are the two most important secrets to making $ERIOUS MONEY online:

Secret #1: Choose Your Weapons Carefully

Whereas many offline companies in the same sector sell identical products and services as other businesses but can still compete through better location, price, promotions, customer service, marketing etc., online companies are different. Because all online companies are basically competing in the same 'neighborhood' the most important prerequisite to be successful online is to provide a product or service that is popular enough to be profitable (seems obvious, eh?).

Therefore, nothing has a bigger influence on your success, than the choice of what you decide to sell or the customers you target.

The best designed website or marketing strategy or affiliate program will not mean a thing if no one wants to buy what you have got to sell.

Today, thanks to my advice and the techniques I will show you, you can identify profitable products or services that will sell well online.

Secret #2: Find Your Pot of Gold

> *"The only way left to make serious money online seems to be by selling a product or service that appeals to an under-serviced but profitable niche."*
>
> *Rich Wiseman*

That statement may also seem obvious but unlike traditional commerce, if you can't compete with huge multinational brands, then you'd better find a product or service that no one else is selling online or a niche market that no one is servicing; a 'pot of gold' no one else has yet found. The truth is if you choose a high demand product or service that fulfills a high-demand, under-fulfilled niche, you can expect to make serious money, very quickly.

Now that e-commerce is mature enough to have countless different businesses competing in most commercial sectors, the best way to ensure a profitable online business is to identify and dominate a profitable and previously under-serviced market sector.

As with any business, if you discover a niche before any serious competitor, then you have a greater chance of capturing the largest market share and gaining 'first-mover advantage'. Fortunately, most online market sectors can be segmented into a niche market sector, as you will see from the companies highlighted in the *Strategic Fit Matrix*™ (see page 47).

To concentrate your business operation on one market niche means to specialize in that specific sector. Consequently, the more you specialize, the more you reduce your prospective customer base.

Obviously, this means that rather than appealing to the broad spectrum of all internet users, your products or services will only appeal to a select, specific customer. However, if that niche has fewer direct competitors, it does have the potential to be profitable. If it is profitable and offers the opportunity for repeat sales, multiple sales, up-sales, cross-sales, and complimentary goods sales, then it should be extremely profitable – it is up to you to exploit it!

> *"If you can dream it, then you can achieve it."*
>
> *Zig Ziglar*

CAN YOUR HOBBY MAKE YOU RICH?

Imagine making money from your hobby or doing something you really enjoy doing. Wouldn't that be a wonderful, life-changing event?

> *"Choose a job you love, and you will never have to work a day in your life."*
>
> *Confucius*

Imagine stress-free living and looking forward to starting work every day; not wanting to go to bed because you enjoy what you do so much.

> *"Some people find an interest in making money, and though they appear to be slaving, many actually enjoy every minute of their work."*
>
> *Walter Annenberg*

It's an advantage if the business you get into is not just one that you think will make money; after all, you have to maintain enthusiasm in your business to maintain growth.

> *"The greatest happiness comes from being vitally interested in something that excites all your energies."*
>
> Walter Annenberg

With enthusiasm comes knowledge, with knowledge comes expertise.

If you have a passion and expertise in a subject then you will put in more hours, and customers will enjoy your enthusiasm and pay for your knowledge and expertise. These are potent ingredients for any successful, enjoyable business.

> *"Making money is a hobby that will complement any other hobbies you have, beautifully."*
>
> Scott Alexander

This is the perfect combination for a successful business idea:

1. **Demand** (enough internet users are interested in the subject to provide a sufficiently large potential customer base)
2. **Expertise** (a product, service, or subject you know in depth)
3. **Passion** (something you have had a deep passion for or interested in for a long time)

1. Demand

If there isn't sufficient demand for your information, products services to make your business idea profitable, then it doesn't matter how passionate, or what level of expertise you have, you simply won't make money.

2. Expert Knowledge

Obviously, if you are an "expert" in a particular subject then potential buyers will perceive you as an authority in the subject and will be happy to pay higher fees for your information, products, or services.

To be a trusted authority in your niche is a huge advantage, so when possible, always try to enter a new niche as an expert. By the way, to be an "expert" only means that you must know your subject one level above your audience or client.

3. Passion

The Passion Principle: **N + P + D = $erious Money***

* N = niche, P = passion, D = demand for product or service.

Without a passion for what you do, you will soon falter and so will your business. After all, potentially, you may have to spend 12 to 18 hours every day working on your business, often for the first one or two years.

> *"Without passion you don't have energy, without energy you have nothing."*
>
> *Donald Trump*

You must constantly be thinking about ways to improve and grow your business, as well as talking about it to everyone, everywhere. If you start a venture that you are not passionate about it will be difficult to put in the hours and energy to make it successful.

> *"The more I want to get something done, the less I call it work."*
>
> *Richard Bach*

What are you passionate about? Try listing all the things you are interested in, then make a list of the things on that list that you are passionate about. Then prioritize; what are you most passionate about? Know who you are; know your strengths and weaknesses, know that you are ready, willing, and able to invest the time, energy, and money necessary to make your venture a success.

> *"Pleasure in the job puts perfection in the work."*
>
> *Aristotle*

Let us say your passion is photography. People pay for solutions to a problem; therefore, you need to find out which problems photographers have and how to solve or alleviate one of these problems. The best place to do this is to research the photography forums and evaluate the needs of your potential customers. Obviously, if you are interested in this area, you will no doubt share many of the frustrations, needs, and wants with other enthusiasts.

For example, imagine you chose underwater or waterproof digital cameras, as used by sports enthusiasts, holiday makers and scuba divers etc. as the product you're really enthusiastic and knowledgeable about - this might make a good choice of online business. The more you specialize in this specific niche the more likely you are to be successful.

> *"Without passion man is a mere latent force and possibility, like the flint which awaits the shock of the iron before it can give forth its spark."*
>
> *Henri Frederic Amiel*

Note: Passion is good. Although, you do not have to be passionate about the audience, niche, or product you choose to promote. Instead, you can be passionate about any part of the process. For example, if you enjoy website design, copywriting, conversion, sales psychology, SEO, marketing etc. then one or more of these can be the motivation and reward you derive from selling online.

WHICH NICHE WOULD SUIT YOU?

Choosing a niche that in some way suits you would be a huge advantage. Ask yourself what are Your Passions, Skills, Experiences, Expertise, Actions and Personality Traits?

Your Passions:

- What do you love to do?
- What work would fit you perfectly?
- If you could do something all day, what would it be?
- When do you feel most fulfilled?

Your Skills:

- What are you good at doing?
- What have you been good at since you were a child?
- What do people always compliment you on?
- What skills have you used most throughout your career?
- What skills have you used the most in your personal life?

Your Experiences:

- What obstacles have you successfully overcome and how?
- Which of your life experiences could benefit others?
- What are three things about you that are memorable?
- Of what do you have unique experience?

Your Expertise:

- What is your education?
- What are your career highlights?
- If you could write a how-to book, what would it be about?
- Of what do you have unique knowledge?

Your Actions:

- What do YOU look for online?
- How often?
- What do you BUY online?
- How much do you SPEND?
- Are there other people like you?

Your Personality:

- Are you an introvert or extravert?
- Who is attracted to you?
- Who asks for your advice?
- Who are you most drawn to work with?
- Who would most benefit from you?

Lastly, ask people close to you what they think you would be good at. This is often the most interesting, revealing, and insightful feedback you will get. You might be surprised how willing people are to tell you what they think of you, and that they know you better than you know yourself!

CHAPTER TWO
IDEA GENERATION (IDEATION)

If you have not got a hobby, or are not passionate about something, then maybe you have got an outstanding idea for a product or business.

"As long as you're going to be thinking anyway, think big."

Donald Trump

Most people who come up with a great idea for a business do so by thinking about their own lives and what product or service they wish was available to them that would make their lives better. Another common way of identifying a gap in any market is when a product or service you want is not available online.

"Necessity... the mother of invention."

Plato

Think simple. Great ideas are often the simplest ones. By thinking of your simplest recurring need, and how you can fulfill it, you can come up with a business idea that also fulfills the needs of others like you.

If you have a business idea, do not try to develop it around what you think potential customers will like or need. Instead, find out what people want or need. Too often business owners get an idea in their head and jump right in with both feet. However, they soon find out that their target market does not want what they are offering.

Talking to potential customers may lead you to the perfect idea. Knowing what potential consumers need and building products to meet those needs is good business practice.

Try brainstorming with other people; talk to family, friends, colleagues etc. See if anyone else has any great ideas. They may not be starting a business, or own one, but they may have a great idea for one. Getting input from other people can help as they may well end up being your customers.

> *"A person with a new idea is a crank until the idea succeeds."*
>
> *Mark Twain*

Research online. Try to research online what others who have a business have done. You may find a great idea or technique that has not been used in your chosen sector. Or, if you have no idea what kind of business to start, try looking online and finding success stories. There may be a great idea or a franchise you can start.

You can then test the idea out to see if there is enough demand for that product or service to make it a profitable proposition. If you do have a great business idea that becomes successful it could make you rich indeed, especially if you fully exploit your first-mover advantage.

> *"If you want to be successful, it's just this simple. Know what you are doing. Love what you are doing. And believe in what you are doing."*
>
> **Will Rogers**

NEVER BE THE FIRST THROUGH THE DOOR

The first person through the door gets shot; the guys that follow learn from that mistake.

> *"In the modern world of business, it is useless to be a creative, original thinker unless you can also sell what you create."*
>
> **David Ogilvy**

Don't be a vanguard, unless it's a simple, easily-fulfilled service or you've got enough money and infrastructure behind you to educate your prospective customers and fulfill their demands, as well as provide spare parts and/or the after-sales service required to support your product or service.

New products or services are rarely successful since your potential customers must be educated as to the benefit to them. Initially, there will not be a network of support systems or services, replacement parts, repair shops etc. to back up your invention. Also, producing products in enough numbers to be profitable is costly and marketing them can be extremely expensive, until sufficient customers use it.

"It is the framework which changes with each new technology and not just the picture within the frame."

Marshall McLuhan

Neither Microsoft, Apple, Google nor eBay invented anything. Nor did they create the sector they dominate. They just made their product or service at least 1% better than their competition. Rather than come up with a completely new idea, research what people are looking to purchase now and give it to them cheaper, quicker, with better customer service and with more added value.

TO TEST IS BEST

"Success depends upon previous preparation, and without such preparation there is sure to be failure."

Confucius

Researching your subject, testing different offers, and measuring responses are the proven tools to uncovering the truth about what your potential customers really want.

"As a small businessperson, you have no greater leverage than the truth."

John Greenleaf Whittier

Do you think you have come up with a unique idea for a product or service that will sell well online? A risk or feasibility study is a well-proven course to take to accurately predict if that idea will be successful.

Feasibility Study Process:

1. Idea > Research > Test > Survey > Research > Feedback > Write Copy > Test > Design Website > Test > Feedback > Review > Changes > Test.

2. If the feedback is positive, write a business plan and add a selling infrastructure (e.g. bank account, credit card processing, more stock, delivery, and fulfillment etc.)

3. Develop a selling strategy: loss leader, up-selling, cross-selling, repeat selling, bundling products, complementary goods and services, affiliate products etc.

> *"Business, more than any other occupation, is a continual dealing with the future; it is a continual calculation, an instinctive exercise in foresight."*
>
> *Henry R. Luce*

WHAT SHOULD YOU SELL?

How can you tell if your business idea is right for the internet? It depends upon what you sell. If you already have a business or are contemplating starting an online business, you need to look at your products and/or services to decide if they fit the internet model of buying. **Not everything sells well online.**

People buy products online that they do not need to smell, touch, or examine. They want products that they are familiar with or products that do not carry an element of surprise upon receiving them. In other words, they have a fairly good idea of what it is they are getting.

For example, online bookstores like Amazon.com do well because those buying a book do not need to hold the book to know something about it. Plus, online bookstores offer feedback that offline bookstores do not, such as reviews, ratings, and extensive descriptions. Add to this fast and easy shipping and you have found a market and retail model that works well online. This same concept also holds true for generic goods such as music, DVDs, electronic goods etc.

Another example is travel; using the internet is easier than making a trip to a travel agency. If you are going on a cruise you can view photos and floor plans, see photos from various excursions, get price quotes, and sailing dates. You can even compare prices with several agencies and then book your cruise online. You know exactly what you should be getting.

Items that are hard to find elsewhere also sell well online. If you offer a unique product that cannot be found in stores, people are more likely to purchase through your website. It makes sense that common products that you can buy at the local store don't sell well online, but if you can identify unique products and advertise those products to their target markets you may have a winner. Also, unique, rare, authentic, or specialized products and services are always popular online (see Strategic Fit Matrix™ page 47).

YOU WON'T GO FAR WITHOUT IPR

If you have generated a unique money-making idea or invention, then you should protect it from being copied or abused by competitors. Whatever your idea is, protect it and make use of it as quickly as possible.

Copyright

If you produce anything that is unique and creative, be it software, an image, a book, or music, you can immediately and automatically have copyright over it; you don't need to register it, you just need a means of dating it to prove you created it first. Also, you can legally protect your creativity against anyone who uses it without your permission.

Patents

Patents (www.uspto.gov/patents/index.jsp) are used to protect inventions such as a physical machine that solves a problem or provides a unique solution. To be granted a patent you will have to prove that the invention is useful and unique and provide detailed drawings of its design.

Trademarks

A Trademark (www.uspto.gov/trademarks/index.jsp) is a mark under which you trade your goods and services e.g. a logo. You can add a "TM" symbol after your business, product etc. to reserve it, or you can use the "®" symbol once you have legally registered your trademark.

"Intellectual property has the shelf life of a banana."

Bill Gates

CHAPTER THREE

SO WHAT EXACTLY DO PEOPLE WANT?

One of the best ways to determine what to sell is to find products that meet the basic needs of people. The good news is that what people need and want will probably remain the same for the rest of your lifetime. The technology for delivering those needs and wants may change but human desires will not.

Therefore, theoretically, all you need to do is figure out what people want, and you can profit from their desires. And, since their desires are predictable, your ability to make money from your ideas just got a lot more bankable as well.

So, what exactly do people want? Abraham Maslow came up with a theory over 50 years ago that still stands today, known as *Maslow's Hierarchy of Needs*. It has become one of the most popular and often-cited theories of human motivation.

Hierarchy of Needs (1990's eight-stage model based on Maslow)

- **Transcendence**: helping others to self-actualise
- **Self-actualisation**: personal growth, self-fulfilment
- **Aesthetic needs**: beauty, balance, form, etc
- **Cognitive needs**: knowledge, meaning, self-awareness
- **Esteem needs**: achievement, status, responsibility, reputation
- **Belongingness and Love needs**: family, affection, relationships, work group, etc
- **Safety needs**: protection, security, order, law, limits, stability, etc
- **Biological and Physiological needs**: basic life needs - air, food, drink, shelter, warmth, sex, sleep, etc.

Maslow explains that humans must fulfill need number one before they will consider need number two, and so on. A person will not try to fulfill needs higher up the pyramid because the initial desires are required for survival.

Maslow suggests the following needs:

1) **Physiological**: hunger, thirst, bodily comforts, etc
2) **Safety/security**: to keep out of danger
3) **Belongingness and Love**: to affiliate with others or be accepted
4) **Esteem**: to achieve, be competent, gain approval and recognition
5) **Cognitive**: to know, to understand, and explore
6) **Aesthetic**: appreciating symmetry, order, and beauty
7) **Self-actualization**: to find self-fulfillment and realize one's potential
8) **Self-transcendence**: to connect to something beyond the ego or to help others find self-fulfillment and realize their potential.

Our three highest-level needs (6, 7 and 8) are satisfied by: money, sex, and food (not necessarily in that order).

Therefore, there will always be a market for websites with any subject that helps the customer become more attractive to the opposite sex (e.g. dieting, clothes, or make up) or that helps people to make money. Also, websites such as dating agencies and cooking are always popular. These needs will never change, ever. So, if you have an idea that fits in one of those categories, and if it is a new spin on existing ideas, you are highly likely to be successful.

If you fulfill a customer's self-actualization (number 7 on the Hierarchy of Needs) and allow them to find self-fulfillment and realize their potential, then you have tapped into the pervading psychology of the new consumer that dominates online.

> *"Human behavior flows from three main sources: desire, emotion, and knowledge."*
>
> *Plato*

To get an interesting insight into people's real dreams, wants, and needs visit www.43.com. Click on "Zeitgeist", then "Goals" to see the top 10 goals for today, for all time, new goals, and achieved goals. Each list of goals has a "See more" link, so you can increase the list to show the top 100. You will notice hundreds of goals that match the list of purchasing motives below.

DO YOU FULFILL YOUR CUSTOMERS' NEEDS?

Here are some purchasing motives that fit into Maslow's hierarchy. These motives are shown in descending order of need. They include:

1. To make money
2. To save money
3. To save time
4. To avoid effort or make work easier
5. To be more comfortable
6. To achieve greater cleanliness/hygiene
7. To be healthier
8. To be pain free
9. To gain praise
10. To be popular
11. To attract the opposite sex
12. To keep/safeguard your possessions
13. To have more fun
14. To satisfy curiosity
15. To protect your family
16. To be in style
17. To acquire new/beautiful possessions
18. To quench your appetite
19. To emulate others

20. To avoid trouble
21. To avoid criticism
22. To be an individual
23. To protect your reputation
24. To grab opportunities
25. To be safe

Since these motives are related to the needs and desires of people everywhere, choosing a business model, product, or service related to any of the 25 needs above will give you a better chance of having a successful online business.

DOES YOUR BUSINESS IDEA FIT THE INTERNET?

Now that you know what sells online, it is time to determine if your business model fits the characteristics needed for selling online. This is known as *Strategic Fit*™. As a small business owner/manager, determining whether your business has the correct *Strategic Fit*™ for e-commerce will be one of the most critical judgments you will make.

The fact is, if you know in advance that your business concept doesn't have the products, services, or processes necessary to be successful online, wouldn't it be sensible to either fix those deficiencies or concentrate on a different channel to market?

Strategic Fit™ Checklist

Does your business...

1. Appeal to the internet audience
2. Provide a genuinely valuable or useful product or service
3. Establish a buyer-seller relationship and trust
4. Use technology judiciously
5. Focus on customer's convenience
6. Provide an exclusive, bespoke, or specialized product or service
7. Save the customer money
8. Provide products or services difficult to acquire elsewhere
9. Add value; provides info about products or services; is entertaining or makes purchasing more pleasurable
10. Have structures in place to cope with any potential demand

Using the *Strategic Fit Matrix™* (see page 47) we can take various random businesses from various niches and test whether they have the *Strategic Fit™* for e-commerce.

#	Business	Website	Category
1.	Antenna Balls	(www.antennaballs.com)	promotions
2.	Book Swim	(www.bookswim.com)	book sales
3.	Card Stix	(www.cardstixcollection.com)	greeting cards
4.	Hungry Pod	(www.hungrypod.com)	music services
5.	Kanda Systems	(www.kanda.com)	electronic sales
6.	Moms on Edge	(www.momsonedge.com)	parenting
7.	Positives Dating	(www.positivesdating.com)	dating/relationships
8.	Racewax.com	(www.racewax.com)	sporting goods
9.	Spreadshirt.com	(www.spreadshirt.com)	clothing
10.	The Merrick Mint	(www.merrickmint.com)	coins/collectibles

Note: companies with a score of 7½ or less do NOT have the correct strategic fit for e-commerce. Obviously, businesses can change their configuration to optimize their systems for the internet.

Strategic Fit Matrix (0 = poor strategic fit; ½ = partial strategic fit; 1 = good strategic fit)

Checklist	Spread Shirt	Hungry Pod	Positives Dating	Kanda Systems	Book Swim	Race Wax	Antenna Balls	Card Stix	Moms on Edge	Merrick Mints
Appeals to Internet audience	1	1	½	½	1	½	½	½	½	½
Provides a genuinely valuable or useful product or service	1	1	1	1	1	1	1	1	1	1
Establishes a buyer-seller relationship & trust	1	1	1	½	1	1	½	½	1	1
Uses technology judiciously	1	1	1	1	1	1	1	1	1	1
Focuses on customer's convenience	1	1	1	½	1	1	1	1	1	1
Provides an exclusive, bespoke or specialized product or service	1	1	1	1	0	1	1	1	1	1
Saves the customer money	½	0	0	½	1	½	0	1	0	½
Provides products or services difficult to acquire elsewhere	1	1	1	1	0	1	1	1	0	1
Adds value; provides info about products or services; is entertaining or makes purchasing more pleasurable	½	0	1	½	1	½	1	½	1	1
Has structures in place to cope with any potential demand	1	1	1	1	1	1	1	1	1	1
Score (out of 10)	9	8	8½	7½	8	8½	8	8½	7½	9

As a small business, you are not likely to be a "Wal-Mart of the Internet." Instead, you will probably operate with a small number of products or services, aimed at a relatively small market; in comparison to the 1 Billion internet shoppers currently available (200+ million in the USA). You are also likely to have a greater need for a competitive edge since you will be competing with others with similar businesses.

> *"The key to competing and surviving against Wal-Mart is to focus your business into a niche or pocket where you can leverage your strengths."*
>
> *Michael Bergdahl*

If the product or service, your company has to offer does not appeal to the current internet audience then setting up an internet presence will only serve as a frustrating drain of your cash. That is why it is necessary to understand who uses the internet and who is buying what.

According to recent research, the percentage of men and women users is essentially the same, as are the differences among races. The biggest differences lie in income and education. Therefore, to have the highest number of potential shoppers, your products or services should be aimed at educated individuals with an income of $75K or higher.

Also, targeting this higher income customer will allow you to charge premium prices and ensure sufficient profit margins. Obviously, consideration should be made as to whether your business idea will "fit" this affluent audience.

INTERNET USAGE AMONG AMERICANS

Percentage of Use in Each Group:

Total Adults	Age	Race/Ethnicity	Geography
Women 70%	18-29 87%	White, Non-Hispanic 73%	Urban 73%
Men 71%	30-49 83%	Black, Non-Hispanic 62%	Suburban 73%
All Adults 78%	50-64 65%	English-speaking Hispanic 78%	Rural 60%
	65+ 32%		

Income (Household)	Educational Attainment
Less than $30,000/yr 55%	Less than High School 40%
$30,000-49,999 69%	High School 61%
$50,000-$74,999 88%	Attended Some College 81%
$75,000+ 93%	College+ 91%

Source: U.S. Census Bureau 2013

WHAT SELLS ONLINE

So, which businesses have the correct "fit" for internet commerce? The obvious candidates for successful e-commerce are simple, recognizable products or services that are easily understood.

Top 10 Products Purchased Online (2013):

1. Women's Apparel
2. Books
3. Computer Hardware
4. Computer Software
5. Toys/Video Games
6. Videos/DVDs
7. Health and Beauty
8. Consumer Electronics
9. Music
10. Jewelry

Note: the thing that most people search for online is information.

Once you determine the product or service you want to sell, then you must consider whether your target market is large enough to be profitable.

WHAT DOESN'T SELL ONLINE

The following list highlights those internet promotions that do **not** have the *Strategic Fit*™ for e-commerce:

1. Generic products or services freely available, easily obtainable, and for the same price elsewhere
2. Products or services that do not appeal to the internet audience
3. New products that are not understood by prospective buyers
4. Products that need pre-sales service to explain the benefits
5. Products that disregard the customers' needs
6. Products limited by their geographical range
7. Product promotion that annoys customers with uninteresting information
8. Websites that download slowly because of excessive use of technology
9. Businesses that misjudge the value customers give to a product
10. Businesses that fail to enhance the product or service with added value and information

HOW CAN YOU MAKE MONEY ONLINE?

Most research suggests that there are basically three ways to make money online:

1. Selling of goods or services
2. Selling advertising (e.g. banner ads, cost per click, or impression, or action etc.)
3. Selling other people's goods or services (e.g. affiliate sales)

If you decide to go online and you have formulated an internet-related business plan, consideration should be made as to what risks you're willing to take and how you're going to measure your success against your objectives.

The costs involved in trading over the internet range significantly, therefore you must evaluate how much you can afford to spend. However, if your products or services fit the internet consumer profile then you may be well on your way to making $ERIOUS MONEY!

THE "BIG THREE" NICHES

1. Health (e.g. wellbeing, diet, fitness etc.)
2. Relationships (e.g. dating, marriage, parenting etc.)
3. Money (e.g. business, career, education etc.)

CONCLUSION

Here I have given you an overview of what it takes to be an online entrepreneur and the importance of finding a profitable niche.

Profit from Persuasion,

Richard G Lewis

Richard G. Lewis
http://www.RichardGLewis.com

If you liked this book you'll LOVE this:
http://www.psychoprofits.com/sales-copy-writing/

ABOUT THE AUTHOR

Richard G. Lewis

Richard G. Lewis is a research psychologist, business consultant and author. Richard helps other business owners, internet marketers and copywriters to understand the power of psychology and persuasion, so they can change their lives for the better and start making a living online.

Since 1998 he has helped develop over 70 e-commerce projects, designing the web architecture, writing the sales copy, and marketing plans for all those brands.

Richard has also written numerous research papers, e-books, and books, including: "Pre Cursor" (2010), "Fortune Cookie" (2009) and the bestseller, "The Small Business Guide to the Internet" (1998).

He has degrees in both Business and Computing. He is also a Fellow of the Chartered Institute of Marketing as well as an expert in e-commerce as recognized by the UK Expert Witness Directory.

Note: Richard is available for consultancy at consultancy@richardglewis.com

Made in United States
Orlando, FL
10 January 2024

42341138R00036